John F. Kennedy

Published by Roaring Brook Press
Roaring Brook Press is a division of Holtzbrinck Publishing Holdings Limited Partnership
120 Broadway, New York, NY 10271
mackids.com

Library of Congress Control Number: 2018956021
ISBN 978-1-250-16894-8

Our books may be purchased in bulk for promotional, educational, or business use. Please contact your local bookseller or the Macmillan Corporate and Premium Sales Department at (800) 221-7945 ext. 5442 or by email at MacmillanSpecialMarkets@macmillan.com.

First published in France in 2018 by Quelle Histoire, Paris
First U.S. edition, 2019

Text: Claire L'Hoër
Translation: Catherine Nolan
Illustrations: Bruno Wennagel, Mathieu Ferret, Nuno Alves Rodrigues, Guillaume Biasse, Mathilde Tuffin, Aurélie Verdon

Printed in China by RR Donnelley Asia Printing Solutions Ltd., Dongguan City, Guangdong Province
10 9 8 7 6 5 4 3 2 1

John F. Kennedy

Roaring Brook Press
New York

Born a Kennedy

John F. Kennedy's family came from Ireland. They immigrated to Boston, Massachusetts, in the 1800s, and soon made a name for themselves in America. John's father, Joseph, became a successful politician and businessman. John's mother, Rose, was the daughter of Boston's mayor, John F. Fitzgerald.

John was born on May 29, 1917, the second of nine siblings. He had a happy childhood, but he grew up knowing that big things were expected of him. After all, he was a Kennedy.

May 29, 1917

Student Days

John went to top schools. He briefly attended Princeton University in New Jersey. Unfortunately, he had to drop out because he was ill. The next year, he enrolled at Harvard University in Massachusetts.

After an injury, John's back began to hurt. He started wearing a brace on his back, which he would need for the rest of his life. Sometimes he had to walk with crutches, too. But John was determined, and he graduated from Harvard in 1940.

1935–1940

War Hero

When the United States declared war on Japan in 1941, John tried to enlist in the military. At first, he was declared unfit because of his poor health. John kept trying. At last, he was allowed to join the navy.

On August 2, 1943, a small boat he was on collided with a Japanese destroyer in the Pacific Ocean. John was badly hurt, yet he swam several miles, leading his shipmates to safety. Later, he received the Navy and Marine Corps Medal for his bravery.

——

1941–1943

Entering Politics

John's father had always wanted one of his sons to shine in politics. His eldest son, Joe, died in the war, so now it was up to John.

In 1946, John ran for the U.S. House of Representatives and won. Then in 1952, he was elected to the U.S. Senate. John seemed to succeed in everything he did. Why not run for president? Although he was still young, he began to consider it seriously.

1946–1952

Meeting Jackie

One evening at a dinner party, John met a smart, elegant woman named Jacqueline Bouvier—better known as Jackie. They fell in love. In the late summer of 1953, John and Jackie got married. Over eight hundred guests were invited to the ceremony, and more than twelve hundred people attended the reception afterward. It was a grand event.

_____

September 12, 1953

Running for President

John decided to run as a presidential candidate for the Democratic Party in 1960. His opponent from the Republican Party was Richard Nixon.

On September 26, John debated Richard Nixon during the first televised presidential debate. John made a much better impression than his rival. He was young and handsome, and he spoke plainly but beautifully. The audience loved him. People nicknamed him "JFK."

On November 8, Americans voted for their next president. John won the election!

———

1956–1960

President of the United States

On January 20, 1961, at age forty-three, John became the youngest U.S. president ever elected. It was a big job. There was a lot of work to be done in the country.

John named his brother Robert attorney general so he could help him fight crime. Robert was determined to put a stop to the Mafia, a group of violent gangsters. John and Robert made many enemies in the criminal world.

John also wanted to end racial segregation. He knew that black citizens should have the same rights as white citizens. Some people were against equal rights. They became John's enemies, too.

1961

Challenges

John faced challenges not only in the States but around the world. Communism, a form of government that the U.S. opposed, was on the rise.

In 1961, Communist authorities decided to build a wall in Berlin, Germany, that would cut the city in two. John visited the city in June 1963. In a famous speech, he said, "*Ich bin ein Berliner*"—"I am a Berliner" in German—to show that he understood the distress of families who lived there.

_____

1961–1963

The Cuban Missile Crisis

The Soviet Union was a powerful Communist country. In October 1962 John learned that the Soviets had placed missiles on the island of Cuba, not far from the U.S. And the nuclear missiles were pointed at America! John sent a warning to the leader of the Soviet Union. He said that the U.S. would attack if the missiles were not removed.

For thirteen days, the world was on edge. Would the U.S. and the Soviet Union go to war? Would they use nuclear bombs and cause terrible destruction?

Finally, the Soviet Union agreed to remove the missiles. The crisis was over.

———

1962

Assassination

On November 22, 1963, John and Jackie went on an official visit to Dallas, Texas. As they drove along the street, the president was shot twice. John was rushed to the hospital, but doctors couldn't save him.

A man named Lee Harvey Oswald was arrested for killing JFK. He did not have time to explain his actions because he was murdered two days after his arrest.

JFK was buried at Arlington National Cemetery on November 25. He remains one of the best-loved American presidents of all time.

―――

November 1963

1917
John is born in Brookline, Massachusetts, on May 29.

1943
John helps save the men in his navy boat during the war.

1952
He is elected to the U.S. Senate.

1915

1940
He graduates from Harvard University.

1946
He is elected to the U.S. House of Representatives.

1953
John marries Jacqueline Bouvier on September 12.

1960
He is named the Democratic presidential candidate.

1961
John launches the Apollo program on May 25, with a mission to send astronauts to the moon.

1962
Famous actress Marilyn Monroe sings "Happy Birthday" to John in May.

1963
On June 26, John gives his famous speech in Berlin.

1963
John is assassinated in Dallas on November 22. He is buried in Arlington National Cemetery three days later.

1961
John becomes president of the United States of America on January 20.

1961
John and his brother Robert begin their fight against organized crime in September.

1962
The Cuban missile crisis begins in October. It ends after thirteen tense days.

1963
John meets with Martin Luther King Jr., an important civil rights leader, on August 28.

1970

John F. Kennedy's Journey

MAP KEY

① Boston, Massachusetts

John was born in a suburb of this big city on the East Coast. His family was well known there. His grandfather, John Francis Fitzgerald, was twice elected mayor of Boston.

② Solomon Islands

It was in this area of the Pacific Ocean that John saved the lives of some of his shipmates after a Japanese attack. He received a medal for his heroic deeds.

③ Washington, DC

When John became president, he and Jackie moved into the White House with their two children, Caroline and John Jr.

④ Berlin, Germany

John went to Berlin, Germany, in 1963. To support the Berliners, whose lives were difficult because of the Berlin Wall, he made a memorable speech.

⑤ Dallas, Texas

John was on an official visit to this city when he was assassinated.

⑥ Arlington, Virginia

John and Jackie Kennedy are buried in this famous military cemetery in Virginia. As a tribute to JFK, an eternal flame burns on his tomb.

United States

Germany

Solomon Islands

People to Know

Joseph Kennedy
(1888–1969)

JFK's father made his fortune in the 1920s and became an ambassador to the United Kingdom in 1938. After World War II, he supported his son's political career.

Jacqueline Kennedy
(1929–1994)

Jackie married John in 1953 and became First Lady of the United States. She was admired for her elegance, taste, and intelligence.

Richard Nixon
(1913–1994)
Richard was the Republican candidate for
president in 1960. John beat him in the first
televised debate, which helped him win the
election.

Robert Kennedy
(1925–1968)
Robert helped his brother John in his political
career, and served as U.S. attorney general.
Like John, Robert was assassinated.

....

....

JFK's father built a family fortune. When John entered Congress, he decided to donate his entire salary to charity. John quietly kept up this practice as president.

John F. Kennedy is the only Catholic president so far.

....

John etched an SOS message into a coconut shell in an attempt to rescue his shipmates during World War II. Later, he had the coconut turned into a paperweight, encased in wood and plastic. It sat on his desk in the Oval Office.

....

JFK began the tradition of having a poet at presidential inaugurations. He asked Robert Frost to recite "The Gift Outright" on his Inauguration Day in 1961. Robert also wrote a whole new poem, entitled "Dedication," for the occasion.

Available Now

 Muhammad Ali

 Marie Antoinette

 Neil Armstrong

 Blackbeard

 Buddha

 Coco Chanel

 Charlie Chaplin

 Cleopatra

 Marie Curie

 Albert Einstein

 Anne Frank

 Gandhi

 Joan of Arc

 Frida Kahlo

 John F. Kennedy

 Martin Luther King Jr.

 Abraham Lincoln

 Nelson Mandela

 Isaac Newton

 Rosa Parks

 Pablo Picasso

 Pocahontas

 Princess Diana

 Vincent van Gogh